OMG Moments: I'm An Adult Already

Serina Mitchner

Copyright © 2020 by Serina Mitchner

All rights reserved. No part of this publication may be reproduced, stored in a retrieval system, or transmitted, in any form or by any means, electronic, mechanical, photocopying, recording or otherwise, without the prior permission of the author.

ISBN: 978-1-945145-98-8

Table of Contents

Author's Note……………………………………page 1

Session 1
Self-Care…………………………………………page 3

Session 2
Inner Beauty……………………………………page 21

Session 3
Attitude…………………………………………page 37

Session 4
Time Management……………………………page 51

Session 5
Money Matters…………………………………page 61

Session 6
Career Readiness………………………………page 69

Reference Section………………………………page 87

Author's Note

Welcome to a book of OMG Moments that will highlight life experiences or reignite old memories of what you experienced. You will take part in lessons that require you to L.I.E. Of course, your eyebrow is raising, and thoughts of possible sin are racing through your mind. This L.I.E. is scary…OMG!!!

Please understand that I am using L.I.E. as an acronym, not to be misconstrued with the word lie – as in not telling the truth, or something false. I created this acronym to allow you to see and hear how you respond and react to words and letter characters.

L – Listen to what is being discussed
I – be Interested in learning
E – be Engaged while reading

My desire is that you take away some positive nuggets that you can apply to your personal and professional life journeys.

On the next page, there will be an activity that will help set the tone for the remainder of the book. I hope I've gotten your attention because now that you're an adult, you're going to need all the information I provide in these chapters. Enjoy reading!

Make a list of three (3) of the most important individuals in your earthly life and explain why they are significant to you.

1) _____

_____

_____

_____

2) _____

_____

_____

_____

3) _____

_____

_____

_____

Session 1:
Self-Care

*"Self-care is giving the world
the best of you,
instead of what's left of you."*

Katie Reed

Oh, my goodness, if in the previous exercise, you did not place **"YOU"** at the top of the list, you might want to consider it in the future. Of course, for the purposes of this assignment, there are not any wrong or right answers. It is for you to discover who you are in this moment. It is rare when individuals make SELF a priority in their lives.

As children, we are always taught to put others first – our parents; siblings; family members; friends. We have even been taught to love our neighbors. Today, the focus will be to learn how to love and acquire the values of being in love with your inward self.

Being in love with your inward self, is your **judgment**, your **evaluation** and your **feelings** about yourself. It is only your opinion of the person who you have existed with since you were born.

Having healthy self-esteem is important to your overall self-confidence. When you don't feel good about yourself, it effects how you look physically, mentally, emotionally, spiritually, and financially. In fact, it can affect how productive you are, how you relate to others and how they relate to you.

Feeling good, happy, and satisfied about yourself are only a few adjectives that describe some parts of high self-esteem to include thinking and believing you are capable of achieving anything. It is when you have high energy, a focus mindset, confidence, and persistence that you thrive into your personal successes at any time.

The opposite of high self-esteem is low self-esteem, which is when you don't feel positive about yourself and when you think you are unworthy of good things happening to you. Also, it is when you focus on your flaws instead of paying attention to your natural gifts. Low self-esteem feeds into negative thinking and makes you believe harsh comments that others make about you. This can cause you to lose confidence. It is essential to eliminate undesirable thoughts when you want to build positive self-esteem.

Our main goal is to build and absorb more about self. Even if this seems difficult, remember that something which appears to be difficult simply requires dedicated effort. As of today, start each day with amazing thoughts about self and kind compliments to another individual. Simple thoughts or communicated compassion for self and others can be your way to make others smile. As long as you do something inspiring and discover things about yourself daily, you will begin to feel better about yourself. Watch your self-esteem level rise higher. And before you know it, you will find that you actually not only like yourself, but you truly love yourself.

Earlier in the chapter, I discussed judgement, evaluation and feelings. Using the definitions below, jot down how you use each to define yourself.

Judgment – The ability to make considered decisions or come to sensible conclusions.

_____
_____
_____
_____
_____
_____
_____
_____
_____
_____

Evaluation – To assess using the amount, number or value of something.

_____
_____
_____
_____
_____
_____
_____
_____
_____
_____

Feeling – An emotional state or reaction.

_____
_____
_____
_____
_____
_____
_____
_____
_____

Measure your self-esteem by taking the assessment.

The Self-Esteem Test

Please mark (T) for True and (F) for False

1. _____ I believe other people are more fortunate than me.
2. _____ I am happy with myself.
3. _____ I don't feel guilty about doing or saying what I want.
4. _____ I always speak up for myself and express my perception.
5. _____ I don't need others to tell me when I have done something good.
6. _____ Being myself is important.
7. _____ I don't care what others think of my views.
8. _____ I can accept constructive criticism without feeling bad.
9. _____ Whenever I make a mistake, I can openly admit it.
10. _____ I deserve love and respect.
11. _____ I never hide my true feelings.
12. _____ I feel needed and valued.
13. _____ I am a happy-go-lucky person.
14. _____ I make friends easily.
15. _____ I don't need others' approval to feel good.
16. _____ I like socializing.

Test Score:

Total number of "True" answers you gave, each is worth one (1) point.

15-16 Points – You have a high level of self-esteem!

12-14 Points – Not bad, there is room for you to improve

8-11 Points – Low self-esteem may be hold you back

Below 8 Points – Your self-esteem is drastically low!

If you received a low score, don't worry; the aim of this course is to help you get to a healthy level by learning to love you!

Twelve steps to developing positive self-esteem

Step One:

Your first competitor is self. Always think and act on ways to better self. Do not even consider comparing yourself with other individuals. There will always be some people who have more than you and some who have less. If you play the comparison game, you'll run into many "opponents" you can't defeat. Be grateful in your own being.

Step Two:

You are responsible for uplifting self. Always know that what you think manifests. Discontinue putting down inner self. You cannot develop high self-esteem if you repeat negative phrases about yourself about yourself and your abilities. Whether speaking about your appearances, your career, your relationships, your financial situation, or any other aspects of your life, avoid self-deprecating comments.

Step Three:

Accept all compliments with the reply of "thank you" only. Have you ever received a compliment and replied, "Oh, it was nothing." When you reject a compliment, you send the message that you are not worth of praise. Again, respond to all compliments with a simple "Thank You" or "How kind of you."

Step Four:

Use affirmations to enhance your self-esteem. On the back of a business card or small index card, write out a statement such as "I like and accept myself" "or I am valuable, lovable person and deserve the best in life." Carry the card with you. Repeat the statement several times during the day, especially at night before going to bed and after getting up in the morning. Whenever you say the affirmation, allow yourself to experience positive feelings about your statement.

Step Five:

Take advantage of workshops, books and cassette tape programs on self-esteem. Whatever material you allow to dominate mind will eventually take root and affect your behavior. If you watch negative reality and television programs or read newspaper articles of murders and business rip off; you will cultivate a cynical and pessimistic mindset. Similarly, if you read books or listen to programs, that are positive in nature, you will take on these optimistic and dutiful characteristics.

Step Six:

Associate with positive and supportive people. When you surround negative people in your personal space that constantly put you and your ideas down, your self-esteemed lowered. On the other hand, when you are accepted and encourage, you feel better about yourself in the best possible environment to raise your self-esteem.

Step Seven:

Make a list of your past successes. It can include your "minor victories," like learning to skate, graduating from high school, receiving an award or promotion, reaching a business goal, etc. Read the list often. While reviewing it, close your eyes and recreate the feelings of satisfaction and joyfulness you experience when you first accomplished each success.

Step Eight:

It is essential to list positive qualities about yourself that you want to live by publicly. Are you honest? Unselfish? Helpful? Creative? Be generous with yourself and write down at least 20 positive qualities. Again, it is important to review this list often. Some people dwell on their shortages and wonder why life is not working out for them. Start focusing on your positive traits and you will stand a much better chance to achieve your desired plans.

Step Nine:

Start giving more by sharing a compliment, including sharing old clothes, cleaning out the pantry, and visit sick or geriatric patients. Money is welcome too. When you do things for others, you are making a positive contribution and you begin to feel more valuable, which, in turn, lifts your spirits and raises your own self-esteem.

Step Ten:

Get involved in work and activities you love. It's hard to feel good about yourself if your days are spent in work you despise. Self-esteem flourishes when you are engaged in work, and activities that you enjoy and make you feel valuable. Even if you can't explore alternative career options at the present time, you can still devote leisure time to hobbies and activities, which you find stimulating and enjoyable.

Step Eleven:

Be true to yourself. Live your identifiable life- not the life others have decided is best for you. You will never gain respect and feel great about yourself when you are not leading the life you want to lead. When make decisions based on getting approval from friends and relatives, you are not being true to yourself and your self-esteem can be challenge to lower level.

Step Twelve:

Take Action! You will not develop high self-esteem if you sit on the sidelines and back away from challenges. When you take action – regardless of the result – you feel better about yourself. When you fail to move forward because of fear and anxiety, you'll be frustrated and unhappy-and you will undoubtedly deal a damaging blow to your self-esteem.

In addition to quizzes and assessments, another way to internalize your true self is through music as it has been known to spark something inside of us.

Listed below are the lyrics to Christina Aguilera's "Beautiful". Whether you read the lyrics, listen to the song or watch the video, you will find something meaningful to improve and empower your inner being. We must remember, a person deserves to be true to himself or herself.

This video could be offensive based on your personal beliefs.

Beautiful

Don't look at me

Every day is so wonderful
And suddenly, it's hard to breathe
Now and then, I get insecure
From all the pain; I'm so ashamed

I am beautiful, no matter what they say
Words can't bring me down
I am beautiful, in every single way
Yes, words can't bring me down`
So don't you bring me down today

To all your friends, you're delirious
So consumed in all your doom
Trying hard to fill the emptiness
The piece is gone, left the puzzle undone
That's the way it is

You are beautiful, no matter what they say
Words can't bring you down
You are beautiful, in every single way
Yes, words can't bring you down
So don't you bring me down today

No matter what we do
(no matter what we do)
No matter what they say
(no matter what they say)
When the sun is shining through
Then the clouds won't stay

And everywhere we go
(everywhere we go)
The sun won't always shine
(sun won't always shine)
But tomorrow will find a way
All the other times

'cause we are beautiful no matter what they say
Yes, words won't bring us down
We are beautiful, in every single way
Yes, words can't bring us down
So don't you bring me down today

Don't you bring me down today
Don't you bring me down today

Now that you have heard the lyrics, determine whether you agree with the statements below…

Christina Aguilera – Beautiful

I am strong and secure.

Every day I am getting better and better

I have the power to realize my goals.

I deserve to succeed

I take charge of my life.

I forgive myself

I am valuable.

I have an inner peace

I stand firmly in my belief in myself.

I heal of all issues affecting my self-confidence.

I am intelligent.

I respect me.

People respect me.

I am confident in myself.

People like me.

I am loveable.

I am a true friend.

I am worthy of love and friendship.

I care for people.

I accept myself completely.

I am confident of my capabilities.

I love and accept all parts of myself.

I am confident.

All false and past images of myself are dissolved.

I am a strong person.

I value and honor myself as I am.

I choose to be happy.

I strive to improve myself.

As we keep living, every day will be different. Our inner beauty will forever evolve as we progress. There are many ways to elevate and strengthen your interior health.

Consider creating an "Enjoy Life" Commitment Calendar for documenting positive affirmations that will make you and others feel amazing. For instance, tell yourself, "I feel good about myself"; "Today I will eat healthy, exercise and take care of my personal hygiene needs." You can also schedule things like "going outside to feel the sunshine on your face"; "calling someone to tell them to make sure you have an amazing day"; "telling your teacher, thank you"; "listening to music with lyrics of substance"; "helping a struggling peer"; "wearing an outfit with your name on it" etc.

When you create this commitment calendar and continue to reinforce a positive self-image, you will see how your inner light glows brighter and how others recognize your beautiful characteristics. Watch how positivity comes your way and how much better you feel! OMG, I'm just saying…TRY IT!

Session 2: Inner Beauty

"Outer beauty will capture the eyes; inner beauty will capture the heart."

Steven Aitchison

Have you ever been mean-spirited to yourself? Do you find yourself thinking, feeling, speaking and acting on phrases like…

I am not trying to do anything.
I do not care.
I am stuck.
I feel terrible.

Words of this sort are detrimental to your inner beauty.

Stop the abuse now! It is imperative for your mindset to change immediately. Self-acceptance is a self-taught process that begins with knowing who you are. It is essential to love yourself from the inside. Your inner beauty reflects your external beauty physically, mentally, and emotionally. It is observed and evaluated by others whether you have good or bad attributes. Be honest with yourself about your body, image, thoughts and feelings so that you can properly set goals and make improvements where necessary. These fundamentals are important to becoming and staying your own best friend.

Complete the activities on the following pages so that you can identify where you are in the quest to love yourself.

List **five** positive characteristics about yourself.

1.

2.

3.

4.

5.

Remember you are your own best friend, write to yourself explaining the things you need to change and the benefits of the change.

Dear Self,

_____
_____
_____
_____
_____
_____
_____
_____
_____
_____

As we discussed in the previous session, a self-esteem assessment is a way to learn more about how you view yourself, which can be a direct reflection of your perceived inner beauty. Self-assessments are another way to broaden the way you think, feel and act. It can be helpful to talk with a career counselor, family and friends about how you plan to improve your inner beauty.

Self-Esteem Quiz

1. Define self-esteem:
    a. How I feel about myself.
    b. How I visualize myself.
    c. How I esteem myself

2. Who has the most influence on establishing your self-esteem as a child?
    a. Friends
    b. Siblings
    c. Parents
    d. Teachers
    e. Employees

3. Esteem should be based on
    a. Money, looks and clothes, career & job
    b. Whether or not someone loves or like you
    c. Your inner qualities
    d. Many achievements, accomplishments and talents
    e. Answer c and d

4. Masks are created to
    a. Substitute for the real self
    b. Bring others closer to us

c. Get us what we want
   d. Make us more genuine and real

5. How to raise self-esteem
   a. Believe in your inner qualities
   b. Be willing to take risk and reveal your true self
   c. Accept weaknesses and learn from mistakes
   d. Don't believe people who put you down
   e. Learn to love yourself
   f. All of the above

6. Is it possible to raise your own self-esteem?
   NO   YES

Label the following characteristics of low and high self-esteem:
A. High Self-Esteem
B. Low Self-Esteem

7. Why try? I could never do it.
8. I admit that I made a mistake.
9. I'm just as good as anyone else.
10. I feel powerless

Listed below are the lyrics to India Arie's "Video". Whether you read the lyrics, listen to the song or watch the video, you will find something meaningful to improve and empower your inner being. We must remember, a person deserves to be true to himself or herself.

This video could be offensive based on your personal beliefs.

Video

[Verse 1]
Sometimes I shave my legs and sometimes I don't
Sometimes I comb my hair and sometimes I won't
Depend of how the wind blows I might even paint my toes
It really just depends on whatever feels good in my soul

[Chorus]
I'm not the average girl from your video
And I ain't built like a supermodel
But I learned to love myself unconditionally,
Because I am a queen

I'm not the average girl from your video
My worth is not determined by the price of my clothes
No matter what I'm wearing I will always be India.Arie

[Verse 2]
When I look in the mirror and the only one there is me
Every freckle on my face is where it's supposed to be
And I know my creator didn't make no mistakes on me
My feet, my thighs, my Lips, my eyes, I'm loving what I see

[Chorus]

[Verse 3]
Am I less of a lady if I don't where panty hose
My momma said a lady ain't what she wears but what she knows...
But I've drawn the conclusion, it's all an illusion
Confusion's the name of the game
A misconception, a vast deception,
Something got to change

Now don't be offended this is all my opinion
Ain't nothing that I'm saying law
This is a true confession
Of a life learned lesson
I was sent here to share with y'all
So get in when you fit in
Go on and shine
Clear your mind
Now's the time
Put your salt on the shelf
Go on and love yourself
'Cause everything's gonna be alright

[Chorus]

[Out]

Keep your fancy drink, and your
expensive minks
I don't need that to have a good time

Keep your expensive cars and your caviar
All I need is my guitar

Keep your crystal and your pistol
I'd rather have a pretty piece of crystal
Don't need your silicone, I prefer my own
What God gave me is just fine…

Now that you've had an opportunity to reflect more deeply about who you are, take a moment to address the questions below.

When you feel lonely and sad:

1. I feel the love of those who are not physically around me.
2. I take pleasure in my own solitude.
3. I am too big a gift to this world to feel self-pity and sadness.
4. I love and approve of myself

When you feel terrified (without your safety being in danger):

5. I focus on breathing and grounding myself.
6. Following my intuition and my heart keeps me safe and sound.
7. I am making the right choices every time.
8. I am drawing from my inner strength and inner light.
9. I trust myself.

When you feel insignificant:

10. I am a unique child of this world.
11. I have every bit as much brightness to offer the world as the next person.
12. I matter and what I have to offer this world also matters.
13. I may be one in 7 billion but I am also one in 7 billion

When you are nervous:

14. I trust my inner light and intuition to guide me.
15. Nervousness surrounding what I want to do is a good sign.
16. I know the situation will work out for my highest good.
17. Wonderful things unfold before me

When you are angry:

18. The anger does not reflect who I am.
19. I let go of my anger so I can see clearly.
20. I accept responsibility if my anger has hurt anyone.
21. I replace my anger with understanding and compassion.
22. I offer a sincere apology to those affected by my anger.

When you feel hopeless and at the end of your rope:

23. I may not understand the good in this situation, but it is there.
24. I can muster up a little more hope and courage from deep inside me.
25. I choose to find hopeful and optimistic ways to look at this.
26. I kindly ask for help and guidance if I cannot see a better way.
27. I refuse to give up because I haven't tried all possible ways.

When you feel conflicted about a decision:

28. I know my inner self will guide me to the right decision.
29. I trust myself to make the best and smartest decision for me.
30. I receive all feedback about a decision with love but make the final call myself.
31. I listen with love to this inner conflict and reflect on it until I get to peace around it.
32. I love my family even if they do not understand me completely.
33. I show my family how much I love them in all the verbal and non-verbal ways I can.
34. There is a good reason I was paired with this perfect family.
35. I choose to see my family as a gift.
36. I grow into a better person from the hardship that I feel with my family.

When you are among friends:

37. I choose friends who approve of me and love me.
38. I surround myself with friends who treat me well.
39. I take the time to show my friends that I care about them.
40. My friends do not judge me, nor do they influence what I do with my life.
41. I take great pleasure in my friends, even if we disagree or live different lives.

When you are around strangers:

42. I am beautiful and smart and that's how everyone sees me.
43. I take comfort in the fact that I can always leave this situation.
44. I never know what amazing incredible person I will meet next.
45. The company of strangers teaches me more about what I like and what I don't like.

When you are at work:

46. I am doing work that I enjoy and find fulfilling.
47. I know that I have a choice in the work that I do in this world.
48. I do not settle for meaningless, boring and frustrating work.
49. I engage in work that impacts this world in a positive way.
50. I believe in my ability to change the world on a small scale with the work that I do.

When you can't sleep:

51. I know that peaceful sleep awaits me in dreamland.
52. I let go all the lies I tell myself.
53. I let go of my thoughts until the morning.
54. I embrace the peace and quiet of the night.
55. I sleep soundly and deeply and beautifully into this night.

When you don't want to face the day:

56. What if this day were to bring me a great joy?
57. I bet today will be a day to remember. Let us go and greet it.
58. My thoughts are my reality and I am thinking of a bright new day.
59. I fill this day with hope and face it with joy.
60. The day will come and go, whether I participate or not. Let us participate.

When you think about your future:

61. I let go of my fears and worries that drain my energy for no good return.
62. I make smart, calculated plans for my future.
63. I enlist the help of experts as needed in my financial planning.
64. I refuse to fall victim in a state of panic by preparing for my future.
65. I trust in my own ability to provide well from my own future.

When you can't get your loved ones to support your dreams:

66. I follow my dreams no matter what.
67. I show compassion in helping my loved ones understand my dreams.
68. I ask my loved ones love me without fully grappling with my dreams.
69. I answer questions about my dreams without getting defensive.
70. I know that my loved ones love me without fully grappling with my dreams.
71. I accept them as they are and continue pursuing my dreams.

When you come face to face with a problem:

72. I am safe and sound.
73. Everything is going to work out for my highest good.
74. There is a great reason that this is unfolding before me.
75. I have the smarts and the ability to get through this.
76. Every problem has a solution, and I seek my solution with resolve.

When you want to do more with your life but feel stuck:

77. I attempt all – not some – possible ways to get unstuck.
78. I seek a new way of thinking about this situation.
79. I know the answer is right before me, even if I am not seeing it.
80. I believe in my ability to unlock the way and set myself free.

When you can't stop comparing yourself to others:

81. I have no right to compare myself to anyone for I do not know their whole story.
82. I compare myself only to my highest self.
83. I choose to see the light that I am to this world.
84. I am happy in my own skin and in my own circumstances.
85. I see myself as the gift I am to my people and community and nation.

When you feel you are not good enough no matter how hard you try:

86. I am more than enough, and I get better every day.
87. I give up the right to criticize myself.
88. I adopt the mindset to praise myself.
89. I see the perfection in all my flaws and all my genius.
90. I fully approve of who I am, even as I get better.
91. I always judge myself to be both good and great.

When you want to give up:

92. I cannot give up until I have tried every conceivable way.
93. Giving up is easy and always an option so let us delay it for another day.
94. I give up the permission to give up for good.
95. It is always too early to give up, so let me give it some more.
96. I must know what awaits me at the end of this rope, so I do not give up.

When you recognize how powerful, gifted, talented and brilliant you really are:

97. The past has no power and no hold over me anymore.
98. I embrace the rhythm and the flowing of my own heart.
99. All that I need will come to me at the right time and place in this life.
100. I am deeply fulfilled with who I am.

http://www.prolificliving.com/blog/2012/08/27/100-positive-affirmations/

Session 3: Attitude

"If you don't like something, change it. If you can't change it, change your attitude."

Maya Angelou

Have you ever awakened or gone to bed mad, upset or disappointed? How about being confused or anxious about something? Have you been in a negative state of mind for an extended amount of time, when you really wanted to be the bigger person who expressed a forgiving attitude for healing purposes? At this very moment, use the three C's to make the necessary modifications: call it, check it, and change it...Immediately!!!! Yesterday is gone. Today is a new day, time, and moment. Allow today to be fused with upbeat, life-filled breaths of joy and happiness.

If you have ever been bent out of shape for being punished for an incomplete assignment delegated by your parents or felt like you were wronged in any way, please make two columns, write down how you were wronged in detail and write down why you feel you are right. What you will find, is that your attitude changes everything.

For instance:

WRONG	RIGHT
Punished for receiving an "F" grade in school	I try to do my best in class

Now take a few minutes to think about the truth and its positivity? If you are still pointing the finger, change everything you are thinking, saying, feeling toward the reflection in the mirror.

What's your attitude?

Put a check in front of the ones that apply to you and see if you need an attitude adjustment!!!

_____I complain about problems rather than doing something about them.

_____Others tell me that I have an attitude problem.

_____I find myself rolling my eyes, sighing under my breath, and pouting when being corrected.

_____I lose my temper when things go wrong on plans get changed suddenly.

_____I am rude and short with people.

_____I use pessimistic language rather than optimistic (faith-filled) language

_____I think that know it all.

_____I am easily irritated or upset

_____I have a "The world owes me" attitude.

_____I look at people for what they can do for me instead of what I can do to help them.

_____I am bothered when someone asks me to do a favor for them.

_____I make decision based on "me" rather than "we".

_____I have a "victim" mentality. For example: "They are treating me like that because I am black, or short, or fat, etc.

Listed below are the lyrics to "Happy" by Pharrell Williams. Whether you read the lyrics, listen to the song or watch the video, you will find something meaningful to improve and empower your inner being. We must remember, a person deserves to be true to himself or herself.

This video could be offensive based on your personal beliefs.

Happy

Here come bad news, talking this and that
(Yeah) Well, give me all you got, and don't hold it back
(Yeah) Well, I should probably warn you I'll be just fine
(Yeah) No offense to you, don't waste your time

Here's why

Because I'm happy
Clap along if you feel like a room without a roof
Because I'm happy
Clap along if you feel like happiness is the truth
Because I'm happy
Clap along if you know what happiness is to you
Because I'm happy
Clap along if you feel like that's what you wanna do

Hey, come on, uh

Bring me down, can't nuthin' (happy)
Bring me down
My level is too high to bring me down (happy)
Can't nuthin', bring me down (happy)
I said, let me tell you now, unh (happy)
Bring me down, can't nuthin', bring me down (happy, happy, happy)

My level is too high to bring me down (happy, happy, happy)
Can't nuthin' bring me down (happy, happy, happy)
I said

Because I'm happy
Clap along if you feel like a room without a roof
Because I'm happy
Clap along if you feel like happiness is the truth
Because I'm happy
Clap along if you know what happiness is to you
Because I'm happy
Clap along if you feel like that's what you wanna do

Because I'm happy
Clap along if you feel like a room without a roof
Because I'm happy
Clap along if you feel like happiness is the truth
Because I'm happy
Clap along if you know what happiness is to you
Because I'm happy
Clap along if you feel like that's what you wanna do

Come on, unh bring me down can't nuthin' (happy, happy, happy)
Bring me down my level is too high (happy, happy, happy)
Bring me down can't nuthin' (happy, happy, happy)
Bring me down, I said

Because I'm happy
Clap along if you feel like a room without a roof
Because I'm happy
Clap along if you feel like happiness is the truth

Because I'm happy
Clap along if you know what happiness is to you, eh eh eh
Because I'm happy
Clap along if you feel like that's what you wanna do

Because I'm happy
Clap along if you feel like a room without a roof
Because I'm happy
Clap along if you feel like happiness is the truth
Because I'm happy
Clap along if you know what happiness is to you, eh hey
Because I'm happy
Clap along if you feel like that's what you wanna do, heh come on

Attitude Self-Assessment Test

This short quiz will help you assess your attitude as it relates to your self-esteem. Rate each of the questions on this four-point scale.

3=always
2=more than half the time
1=occasionally
0=never

1. _____ I feel comfortable when I am set apart from the group.
2. _____ I accept responsibilities when things go wrong.
3. _____ I share credit with others.
4. _____ I am comfortable accepting a compliment.
5. _____ I set goals and visualize accomplishing them.
6. _____ I am confident in myself and my abilities.
7. _____ I am willing to take necessary risks.
8. _____ I think positively in the face of challenges.
9. _____ I can say "no".
10. _____ I understand my attitude towards people plays a role in my success.
11. _____ I see the positive qualities in other people.
12. _____ I listen to others.
13. _____ People describe me as a positive person.
14. _____ I understand my attitude towards circumstances controls how I respond to challenges
15. _____ I view each new situation as an opportunity or a challenge.

Add up the total points and check scoring after the jump:

38-45: High Self-esteem. You are confident about yourself and your liabilities. You have a positive attitude.

30-37: Strong Self-esteem. You are generally confident about yourself and your abilities. You tend to remain positive and optimistic in your attitude.

23-29: Moderate self-esteem. You have periods of self-doubt but tend to be more positive than negative.

15-22: Low self-esteem. You have periods of self-doubt and tend to be more negative than positive.

0-14: Negative self-esteem. You have little or no confidence in your abilities. You tend to demonstrate negative attitudes.

Attribution: http://www.citehr.com/161415-test-your-attitude.html#ixzz1xgSRYi6I

Guidelines for A Positive Attitude

1. Speak positively to yourself. For instance, make comments to yourself like:

   "I'm good."
   "I'm great."
   "I'm doing really well."
   "I am self-confident."
   "I feel good when I speak beautiful things to myself."

   Trust that you are as deserving of these truthful comments. Besides, you do not need to wait for anyone to confirm what you already know. Speak these truthful statements to yourself at any time.

   Be certain to give yourself accolades when you do something good (a decent job at school, help a friend, compliment a stranger, etc.) Pat yourself on the back for a good job well done.

2. Be grateful for everything. For example, you can feel thankful for opening your eyes in the morning, being able to see through your eyes, you see leaves sway on the trees or observe what ingredients are being used to cook breakfast.

   Being thankful for everything puts you in an attitude of appreciation and receiving beauty in return. As a result, you develop and keep a positive mood and feel wholehearted towards whatever comes next.

3. Think about the difficult times in your past and identify at least one good thing that came forth. All events have a positive outcome, even the negative ones. Therefore, it's logical to think that when a difficult event comes along in the future, no matter what it is, you will get something out of it for your own benefit.

   Feel the serenity that knowing this creates and accept that you are able to deal with anything in your life, if you decide so.

4. By acknowledging your personal accomplishments, it affirms positive self-image. Make positive statements to yourself, "I'm good"; "I'm doing extremely well".

   Reflect on the positive qualities that helped you achieve: power, persistence, compassion, etc. Feel worthy about yourself. You possess those gifts and can bring them into play anytime.

5. Keep your main goal in focus. If you do not have a goal in your life, discover one, make it your dream and start manifesting it into reality. For example, some people have a goal of what life will be like financially after retirement, start saving money for an easier living.

   When you get busy working on achieving your main goal you acquire purpose and self-fulfillment, which leads to keeping a positive frame of mind. Your purpose will be identified easily into your life.

Having a Positive Attitude Will Make You A Winner

The world that we see and live in is partially created in our minds from our own thoughts and point of view. The way we feel about ourselves and the things around us, is ultimately the stage that we create inside of ourselves. This is the world of our attitude. Attitude affects so much, and ironically enough, is totally under our control. By consciously changing and monitoring our attitude to find the positive in our life, we can drastically change our lives in the best of ways. This means that even though it may sound cliché, no matter what obstacles life throw at us, we can walk always a winner, all because of a positive attitude. Having a positive attitude is a choice that you and only you make; feeling good does not depend on external circumstances, but on what you choose to think.

Charles Swindoll made an excellent statement about attitude that I love: "The longer I live the more I realize the impact of attitude on my life." Attitude is more important than the past, education, money, circumstances, failures, successes, than what other people think or say or do. It is more important than appearance, giftedness or skill. It will make or break a company, a church, a home. The remarkable thing is that we have choices everyday regarding the attitude we embrace for that day. We cannot change our past. We cannot change the fact that people will act in a certain way. We cannot change the inevitable. The only thing we can do is play on the string we have, and that is our attitude. I am convinced that life is 10% of what happens to us and 90% how we react to it.

When you are having a bad day, or when you feel unattractive, remember there is something you can do about it. No, you can't lose 5 pounds right away, but the one thing that you can change instantly is your attitude about the situation. Starting the positive process flowing will be the thing you need to create a domino effect of a wonderful string of great events happening in your life. All you need to do is take the reins because you are already in control. All you have to do is use the power that you have within you. It is there. Decide today that you are going to make having a positive attitude number one in your life, so that you can spread your positive attitude and confidence to others. Having a positive attitude as a constant in your life will, without fail, makes you a winner in all that you do!

Session 4: Time Management

"Time isn't the main thing. It's the only thing."

Miles Davis

Oh My Goodness! I did not finish my homework by the deadline. I am late for my job interview because I got up 15 minutes late. I did not pass my final exam because I only studied the night before.

Regardless of what you have to do for school, work, your parents, or children, have you ever wondered why it is that you are unable to complete one task successfully? Typically, the solution lies in managing your time effectively and putting in the required work to maintain your schedule.

When it comes to managing your time, there are many tips that can help you better plan. Your time organization will always be unique from that of anyone else.

Listed on the following pages are exercises that can help you better manage your time.

Write a list of "Things to Do". Categorize them by:

- Do Now (Priority)
- Do Next (Urgent)
- Do Later (Necessary)
- Do Never (Unimportant)

_____
_____
_____
_____
_____
_____
_____
_____
_____
_____
_____
_____
_____
_____
_____
_____
_____
_____
_____
_____
_____
_____
_____
_____

Write your tasks by starting every sentence with "I will".

For example:

I will go to bed earlier so that I will have an enormous amount of energy for tomorrow.

I will leave from home at 7:00 a.m. to catch the 7:10 a.m. bus.

I will study in the library on Tuesday evenings between 5pm and 6:30pm.

_____
_____
_____
_____
_____
_____
_____
_____
_____
_____
_____
_____
_____
_____
_____
_____
_____
_____
_____

Consider how you will add 5 or more of these positive activities on your to do list. *Determine which applies for you.*

FY=Family
SS=Siblings
CN=Children
MS=Meals
BE=Bedtime
EL=Email
SL=School
CH=Church
LY=Laundry
SG=Shopping
RG=Reading
CG=Cleaning
HW=Homework
SM=Social Media
PB=Pay Bills
CG=Community Group

_____
_____
_____
_____
_____
_____
_____
_____
_____
_____
_____
_____

This is an assignment that will make you think, think and think, "What am I doing for ME on a daily basis."

The information does not have to be the exact time however, it will show you just how much time you are spending on, with, and for other people, places and things.

Let's get started...

Things to do	12am	1am	2am	3am	4am	5am	6am	7am	8am	9am	10am	11am
	12pm	1pm	2pm	3pm	4pm	5pm	6pm	7pm	8pm	9pm	10pm	11pm

It is important to manage your time because you do not want to be in a pool of quicksand sinking with the other "IFs". You want to choose to do things differently from this day forward. Start NOW!!!

By listing stereotypes in the following categories below, it will help you decide where you fit.

List Stereotypes for the following categories below:

    Women   Men   Children   Friends

1.

2.

3.

4.

5.

Now ask, "Where do I fit in these stereotypes?"

Listed below are several examples of why it is important to manage your time. **Please write how you have managed time in an advantageous or disadvantageous way.**

Advantages of Managing Time

1. Arrive on time for job interview.
2. Studied, prepared and received assistance from instructor before quizzes and exams.
3. _____
4. _____
5. _____
6. _____
7. _____

Disadvantages of NOT Managing Time

1. Late and disqualified for employment.
2. Crammed for exam and received failing grade.
3. _____
4. _____
5. _____
6. _____
7. _____

Session 5:
Money Matters

"You must gain control over your money or the lack of it will forever control you."

Dave Ramsey

Now that you are gainfully employed, it is time to discuss money responsibilities. Be honest, have you ever spent your last $5.00 on eating a Wendy's value meal when you should have kept it for bus fare to school or work? At some point in your young lives, there will be times where a major decision will need to be made that could affect your life personally or possibly involve others within your homes.

In this session, you will learn lessons of basic money principles to include real world scenarios. First, you need to understand the difference in earned vs. unearned income.

Earned income is the monetary benefit you receive for the work or services you perform.

Unearned income is money you receive without actively working or performing a service.

In the chart below are lists of examples:

Earned Income	Unearned Income
• Salaries and Wages	• Child Support
• Commissions	• Social Security
• Bonuses	• Pension
• Tips	• Alimony
	• Dividends
	• Interests
	• Unemployment

Scenario of Money Exercise 1:

In this assignment, you will determine whether you can afford to purchase a new pair of Air Jordan gym shoes for your 16-year-old son who is an Honor Roll Student. You will circle the word **APPROVED** or **DENIED**.

As a single parent, you are not employed. Your unearned income is SSI and Child Support monthly payments. The SSI amount received monthly is $681.00, Link Card $260.00 and Child Support monthly payment is $320.00. Also, you go to the currency exchange to handle your personal business affairs. Your monthly expenses are as follows:

Rent	$550.00
Com Ed	$36.35
People Gas	$42.00
Car Note	$125.00
Car Insurance	$25.00
Life Insurance	$17.00
Prepaid Cell phone	$30.00
Personal Items	$20.00
Basic Cable	$30.00
Phone & Internet	$79.00
Currency Exchange Fees	$5.75
Money Orders	$0.50

What is the total of your monthly income? _____

What is the total of your expenses? _____

Will your son get the shoes he has earned? Circle your decision.

APPROVED   DENIED

What will you do in this situation?

_____
_____
_____
_____
_____
_____
_____

Should you consider opening a bank account? Why or why not?

_____
_____
_____
_____
_____

What can you afford?

_____
_____

Is there any expense missing that I did not include?

_____
_____
_____

Scenario of Money Exercise 2:

In this assignment, you will determine whether ATTEMPTING to SAVE money is relevant. It is almost Christmas and you are going to celebrate. You will circle the word NOW or LATER.

You are single parent and gainfully employed. After taxes, you earn approximately $1,500.00 per pay period. Your monthly income is $3,000.00. You received a $500.00 calendar year bonus for your outstanding work performance. Although you know that the prices will decrease after the holiday, you plan to spend the money on Christmas gifts so that everyone can have a present to open. Your monthly expenses are as follows:

Mortgage	$873.00
Com Ed	$112.35
Nicor	$82.00
Car Note	$445.00
Car Insurance	$60.00
Life Insurance	$17.00
**** *Heating Disaster*	*$785.00* ****
Prepaid Cell phone	$30.00
Personal Items	$20.00
Basic Cable	$89.00
Phone & Internet	$119.00
Groceries	$235.00
Gas	$300.00

What is the total of your monthly income? _____

What is the total of your expenses? _____

When should you go Christmas shopping? Circle your answer.

NOW   LATER

Please explain why you made the decision?

_____
_____
_____
_____
_____
_____
_____
_____
_____
_____
_____
_____
_____
_____
_____

Session 6: Career Readiness

"Choose a job you love, and you will never have to work a day in your life."

Confucius

Oh My Goodness! Growing up can be extremely difficult! Have you or someone you know ever been confused about what the future holds? Are you thinking about how you should have been more focused and serious about your responsibilities? Time out for this F.E.A.R. - **Forget Everything And Run;** instead, I encourage you to *Face Everything And Rise* to the top! At this moment, it is time for you do the work, express your creativity, develop skills, and dream of building your future the way you desire.

Listed below are the lyrics to "Do You Know Where You're Going To?" by Diana Ross. Whether you read the lyrics, listen to the song or watch the video, you will find something meaningful to improve and empower your inner being. We must remember, a person deserves to be true to himself or herself.

This video could be offensive based on your personal beliefs.

Do You Know Where You're Going To?

Do you know where you're going to?
Do you like the things that life is showing you
Where are you going to?
Do you know?
Do you get
What you're hoping for
When you look behind you
There's no open door
What are you hoping for?
Do you know?

Once we were standing still in time
Chasing the fantasies
That filled our minds
You knew how I loved you
But my spirit was free
Laughin' at the questions
That you once asked of me
Do you know where you're going to?
Do you like the things that life is showing you
Where are you going to?
Do you know?

Now looking back at all we've planned
We let so many dreams
Just slip through our hands
Why must we wait so long
Before we'll see
How sad the answers
To those questions can be
Do you know where you're going to?
Do you like the things that life is showing you
Where are you going to?
Do you know?
Do you get
What you're hoping for
When you look behind you
There's no open door
What are you hoping for?
Do you know?

Songwriters: Gerry Goffin / Michael Masser

TAKE ACTION

Right now is time to think about what career you would like to pursue. For you to prepare to be a selected candidate for a position, there are a few required skills you must develop. You must also research interests to learn as much about the company and its current employment opportunity. Let's start!

Exercise #1

List types of positions you would like to be employed as:

1.

2.

3.

4.

5.

Exercise #2

List companies you would like to be employed with and write the reason(s) why.

1. _____
_____
_____
_____

2. _____
_____
_____
_____

3. _____
_____
_____
_____

4. _____
_____
_____
_____

5. _____
_____
_____
_____

Exercise #3

List places you can search for the employment opportunities:

1.

2.

3.

4.

5.

Resume

How to complete a resume step by step:

1. **Type of Resume**: There are several types of resumes used to apply for job openings. Depending on your personal circumstances, an individual might choose a functional, combination or targeted resume. In this lesson book, we are focused on a chronological resume. It is the simplest format of the resumes. It focuses on your key accomplishments and skills rather than your employment history.

2. **Personal Information**: Create a centered header which includes your personal contact information. The information is used by a company's Human Resources recruiter to communicate with you for a potential opportunity.

Name
Address
City, State, Zip Code
Telephone Number
Email Address

3. **Career Objective**: Add a profile which will specify to an employer the employment opportunity in which you have an interest. It is best to apply for a current and available opportunity.

4. **Work Experiences or Skills**: Your work history is most important component of your resume. Employers will want to know where you have gained your work experiences, period you worked there, and duties you held in each role. They will be reviewing your resume to see how your experience matches up with what they are looking for in prospective employees.

- List the jobs, community services and internships you have held in reverse chronological order, with the most recent positions first.

- For each position, include job title, company, location, dates of employment, and a bulleted list of the strongest accomplishments for each job.

5. **Activities:** List activities in which you have participated. This is the place to note membership or leadership in organizations of any kind – churches, athletic teams, etc.

6. **Education:** The education section generally comes next. You need only to list degrees earned, with the highest first, when you have been out of school for a few years.

    The education section of your resume can be listed above your employment history when you are a current student or recent graduate. If you have work experience, list your educational information below the work/employment history section. Education should be listed in reverse chronological order, with the most recent and advanced education first. Include the name of the school, the degree earned, and the date you graduated.

7. **Awards:** Feel free to mention awards and accomplishments you have earned. It is attractive to share with potential employers how you have been recognized by someone else. It will show the employer how qualified you are.

8. **Personal Interests:** In this section, it is a way to show how well-rounded you are. It is about highlighting hobbies that have helped you develop as a person. It is optional; feel free to exclude this section.

Cover Letters

Nowadays, submitting a cover letter is extremely imperative. An employer wants you to apply for current and available positions that have job announcements or a specific title. Companies are working smarter with less staff available.

A cover letter is a one-page document you should include with your resume when applying for an employment opportunity. It is meant for you to introduce yourself to human resources, disclose where you discovered the available opportunity, tell why you should be the selected candidate for the job, and further explain other aspects of your resume. Good, you are ready to homework.

Find out whom you are going to send your cover letter to:

Before introducing yourself to human resources, make every attempt to find out the hiring managers name by researching the company's website, social media such as LinkedIn or making a phone call to inquire about the hiring manager's name. This will eliminate addressing the recruiter as "To whom it may concern" or "Dear Sir or Madame."

Introduce Yourself:

Begin by telling the employer what position you are interested in applying for and how you learned about the current opening. Briefly present information about yourself, your area of experience and career goals, and explain how they will meet the mission of the company.

Sell Yourself:

Describing your previous employment experiences, knowledge, skills and abilities will allow you to demonstrate how you meet the company's essentials. Feel free to go the extra mile by doing research about the company and telling them what you know about their industry. It will help you when you get the interview.

Conclusion:

In your last paragraph, inform them that you would love to be the selected candidate for an interview. Tell them that you look forward to hearing from them within the week and if you do not hear from them to expect your call. Be certain to thank them for taking the time to read your letter.

Job Application

Typically when you apply for a job, completion of an employment application is required even if you have submitted a resume. Employers retain a record of your personal and work history, which is verified and signed by you.

Be certain to have your personal and professional information. Be certain to make a copy of your resume available in PDF and Word formats to view and duplicate the information onto the application. You can store the information in your email, flash drive, cellular phone and/or keep an available hard copy in a folder.

No matter how and where you complete and submit your application, it is important to follow the instructions; complete it accurately and thoroughly without errors. Therefore, practice filling out an application at home before going to a company to get an application in person, applying in person, or filling out the application on-line. It needs to be neat and typed without spelling or grammatical errors.

Be certain to list a minimum of three professional references that you will allow the employer to contact. Before you submit the names, addresses and telephone numbers of your references, make your references aware of the employer who will be contacting them. Often, employers contact references only to discover your reference is not expecting a call.

Lastly, be prepared to take pre-employment assessments along with drug tests. Employers want to benefit from hiring proficient employees.

Dressing for a Successful Interview

Have you ever seen a girl, lady or woman wear an extremely short skirt to work, church, or school? What about a boy, guy or man wearing his pants sagging? What did you say or think? Did you wonder the type of job they were dressed for?

Somewhere this state of being requires an about face to exit out of the company's door before having an opportunity to interview. Appropriate attire is essential to making a grand first impression for your interview. You want to be chosen for employment. Let us discuss how to dress for a job interview.

Generally, professional or business attire is the dress code rule. For men, this means a suit (jacket and slacks), with a collar and button-down shirt and tie, sweater and casual shoes; for women, a dress is appropriate.

Dress for a Successful Interview

You can easily make a great impression based on how you have dressed.

Men	**Women**
Wear a suit Suit Jacket, collared shirt, tie, pants, socks and dress shoes.	Wear a skirt or suit Knee length skirts, solid color blouse, neutral hose and low heel pumps
Avoid flashy colors: Dark Earth Colors: Navy, Black, or Brown	Avoid animal prints, lace, see through attire: Earth Colors: Black and Navy
Hygiene: Shower, Comb Hair, Brush Teeth, Shave	Hygiene: Neat hair, deodorant, no or light polish on short fingernails
Do not: Spray cologne Smoke cigarettes or natural herbs Drink alcohol	Do not: Spray perfume Wear dangling earrings Bling jewelry

Mock Interview Process

Are you nervous? You are getting to ready for an important job interview that will secure you with food, shelter and clothing. For the next 15-20 minutes, you will apply for a position with the company that you are interested in working for. Please complete the **job application** and prepare for your interview. Your interviewer will take notes and be prepared to share the information on behalf of you and vice versa.

Be prepared to answer the following questions:

- Please tell me about yourself.

- Where would you like to be in your career five years from now?

- Can you tell me about your proudest achievement?

- Give me an example of a time when you had to think out of the box.

- What negative thing would your last boss say about you?

- What can you do for us that another candidate cannot do?

- Do you have any questions or comments about the position?

Be prepared for constructive feedback from your mock interviewer using the evaluation form below: https://www.sampletemplates.com/business-templates/evaluation/interview-evaluation-forms.html

A Simple Thank You Goes A Long Way!

Have you ever pondered why you were not considered for an interview? Of course, there could be numerous reasons. Did your background qualifications meet the company's expectations? Did you submit an incomplete application? Were your dates of employment accurate? What about the title of your job? What did your professional references tell your potential employer? Did you express enthusiasm?

You might not ever find out why. Employers will not call or send a letter telling you the reason why you did not make the cut. Most of the time, you have only one opportunity to represent yourself with excellence, which means you should be meticulous when preparing for the entire employment process.

Even if you did receive an interview, have you ever questioned why you were not offered a position afterwards? Did you dress appropriately? Did you tell the company what you knew about their products or services? Did you inform the interviewer that you were interested and would like to be the selected candidate for the position? Did you send a simple "thank you" message?

Let us be certain that you have your final opportunity to reiterate any pertinent details you wish to include by writing your letter of appreciation to the employer. Sending a thank you note is good manners and will keep your name in front of the decision makers. You will be able to remind the interviewer about details you discussed during the interview and reiterate how interested you are in the position.

It is always a great idea to write a thank you letter after interviewing with a company for a job. In fact, some employers look for candidates to send a note as quickly as possible. Sometimes it is a part of their final decision of who might be considered and offered a job. Be certain to take the time to do so, as it will help you to leave your interviewer with an affirmative impression.

Reminder Note:

Sending a thank you note after a job interview is a good way to signal your interest in the role and solidify the interviewer's positive impressions and/or say it verbally.

This can be done through regular mail, email, telephone, and fax. Please do not text.

Reference Section

Jasmine Jeneva Jacksen
12600 South Ashland Street
Calumet Park, IL 60827
(708) 239-5337
JJJacksen@gmail.com

CAREER OBJECTIVE   To obtain a position as Cashier with an aspiring company where I can utilize my strong mathematical skills in operating cash transactions and professional customer service.

EMPLOYMENT HISTORY

McDonalds	**Calumet Park, IL**
Cashier	Jan/2018 – Present

- Receive payments by cash, check, credit cards or automatic debits.
- Issue receipts, refunds, credits, or change due to customers.
- Count money in cash drawers at the beginning of shifts to ensure that amounts are correct and that there is adequate change.

Burger King	**Calumet Park, IL**
Cashier	Jan/2016 – Dec/2017

- Perform basic math functions to collect accurate payments and disburse change.
- Operate registers, scanners, scales and credit terminals
- Maintain accurate cash drawer
- Keep the checkout area clean and orderly

ACTIVITIES

Drama Club: Calumet Elementary	Fall 2018
Baseball Team: 8th Grade Team Captain	Spring 2018

EDUCATION

Alan B. Shepard	**Palos Heights, IL**
Date of Graduation: June 2021	Aug/2017-Present

AWARDS:

Honor Roll, Alan B. Shepard High School, Freshman Year 2017

PERSONAL INTERESTS:

Hockey, lawn care, t-shirt designing, swimming

Sample Cover Letter:

Jasmine Jeneva Jacksen
12600 South Ashland Street
Calumet Park, IL 60827
(708) 239-5337
JJJacksen@gmail.com

John Bell
Ultra-Foods Groceries
12900 South Ashland Street
Calumet Park, IL 60827

RE: Current Cashier Position

Dear Mr. Bell,

I am writing about the current Cashier position posted on your public job board located inside of your store in Calumet Park, IL. As an experienced cashier, I am extremely interested in this job at your store.

As a professional and qualified cashier, I am eager to contribute my abilities and experience to Ultra-Foods Groceries. Given my extensive cashier work history, I believe I can help Ultra-Foods Groceries to meet its goals to providing excellent customer services to its internal and external customers.

Please find my resume attached for your review. Feel free to contact me at (708) 239-5337. I look forward to hearing from you.

Sincerely,

Jasmine Jeneva Jacksen

Enclosures

Please complete the sample job application listed below:

Employment Application   Teens Enrichment & Empowerment Navigation Services, Inc.

Applicant Information

Full Name: _____ Date: _____

           Last   First   M.I.

Address: _____

           Street Address   Apartment/Unit #

_____

           City   State   ZIP Code

Phone: _____ Email _____

Date Available: _____ Social Security No.: _____ Desired Salary: $_____

Position Applied for: _____

Are you a citizen of the United States? YES NO   If no, are you authorized to work in the U.S.? YES NO

Have you ever worked for this company? YES NO   If yes, when? _____

Have you ever been convicted of a felony? YES NO

If yes, explain: _____

91

Education

High School:
_____ Address: _____

From: _____ To: _____ Did you graduate? YES   NO   Diploma :: _____

College:
_____ Address: _____

From: _____ To: _____ Did you graduate? YES   NO   Degree: _____

Other:
_____ Address: _____

From: _____ To: _____ Did you graduate? YES   NO   Degree: _____

References

Please list three professional references.

Full Name: _____ Relationship: _____

Company: _____ Phone: _____

Address: _____

Full Name: _____ Relationship: _____

Company: _____ Phone: _____

Address: _____

Full Name: _____ Relationship: _____

Company: _____ Phone: _____

Previous Employment

Company: _____ Phone: _____

Address: _____ Supervisor: _____

Job Title: _____ Starting Salary: $ _____ Ending Salary: $ _____

Responsibilities: _____

From: _____ To: _____ Reason for Leaving: _____

May we contact your previous supervisor for a reference?   YES   NO

_____
_____

Company: _____ Phone: _____

Address: _____ Supervisor: _____

Job Title: _____ Starting Salary: $ _____ Ending Salary: $ _____

Responsibilities: _____

From: _____ To: _____ Reason for Leaving: _____

May we contact your previous supervisor for a reference?   YES   NO

_____
_____

Military Service

Branch: _____ From: _____ To: _____

Rank at Discharge: _____ Type of Discharge: _____

If other than honorable, explain:
_____

Disclaimer and Signature

I certify that my answers are true and complete to the best of my knowledge.

If this application leads to employment, I understand that false or misleading information in my application or interview may result in my release.

Signature: _____ Date: _____

JOB INTERVIEW EVALUATION FORM

INTERVIEWEE NAME:_____ DATE:_____

All applicants are expected to have an appropriate cover letter and resume. Interviewer: Please place an X in the appropriate box and make comments that would be helpful for the interviewee in improving their interviewing skills.

APPEARANCE	Poor	Fair	Average	Good	Superior
Dress					
Grooming					
Body Language					
Eye Contact					

CHARACTERISTICS	Poor	Fair	Average	Good	Superior
Assertive					
Achievement-oriented					
Cooperative					
Responsible					
Outgoing					
Open					
Dedicated					
Poise					
Maturity					
Professional					
Verbal/Persuasive					
Ability to learn					

GOALS/PERCEPTION OF SELF	Poor	Fair	Average	Good	Superior
Realistic appraisal of self					
Reason for interest in field					
Realistic career goals					

QUALIFICATIONS	Poor	Fair	Average	Good	Superior
Education/Training					
Accomplishments					
Skills					
Relevant Experience					
Potential					

DECISION MAKING/PROBLEM SOLVING	Poor	Fair	Average	Good	Superior
Creativity					
Logic					

REASONS FOR SELECTING PARTICULAR ORGANIZATION	Poor	Fair	Average	Good	Superior
Commitment					
Knowledge of Organization					
Knowledge of Industry					

JOB EXPECTATIONS	Poor	Fair	Average	Good	Superior
Realistic					
Match employer's needs					

LONG TERM OBJECTIVES	Poor	Fair	Average	Good	Superior
Realistic					
Potential to grow					

OVERALL EVALUATION	Poor	Fair	Average	Good	Superior

ADDITIONAL COMMENTS:

Sample Thank You Letter

Jasmine Jeneva Jacksen
12600 South Ashland Street
Calumet Park, IL 60827
(708) 239-5337
JJJacksen@gmail.com

John Bell
Ultra-Foods Groceries
12900 South Ashland Street
Calumet Park, IL 60827

Dear Mr. Bell:

I sincerely enjoyed meeting with you on Monday, January 3, 2018 and learning more about the Cashier position at Ultra Foods Groceries.

Our conversation confirmed my interest in becoming part of Ultra Foods staff. I am particularly pleased at the prospect of being able to use the latest cash registers that is moving with technology advancements.

I feel confident that my experience would enable me to fill the job requirements effectively.

Please feel free to contact me if I can provide you with further information. I look forward eagerly to hearing from you and being the newly hired cashier for Ultra-Food Groceries.

Sincerely,

Jasmine Jeneva Jacksen

Works Cited:

Christina Aguilera. Beautiful. Stripped. 2002. CD

Diana Ross. Do You Know Where You're Going To. Mahogany. 1975. Album

India Arie. Video. Acoustic Soul. 2001. CD

Pharrell Williams. Happy. Despicable Me 2. 2013. CD

www.ingramcontent.com/pod-product-compliance
Lightning Source LLC
LaVergne TN
LVHW061343060426
835512LV00016B/2636

9 781945 145988